Living with
the Rosary

JOSEPHINE LOMBARDI

NOVALIS

© 2013 Novalis Publishing Inc.

Cover design and layout: Audrey Wells
Cover image: Sarah Hall (www.sarahhallstudio.com)
Interior photographs: W.P. Wittman (pp. 6, 10); Ingram (p. 8); Plaisted (pp. 12, 13, 19, 29); Jupiter Images (p. 21); Crestock (pp. 24, 32)

Published by Novalis

Publishing Office
10 Lower Spadina Avenue, Suite 400
Toronto, Ontario, Canada
M5V 2Z2

Head Office
4475 Frontenac Street
Montréal, Québec, Canada
H2H 2S2

www.novalis.ca

Cataloguing in Publication is available from Library and Archives Canada.

ISBN: 978-2-89646-301-5

Printed in Canada.

The Scripture quotations contained herein are from the New Revised Standard Version of the Bible, copyrighted 1989 by the Division of Christian Education of the National Council of the Churches of Christ in the United States of America, and are used by permission. All rights reserved.

All rights reserved. No part of this publication may be reproduced, stored in a retrieval system, or transmitted in any form, or by any means, electronic, mechanical, photocopying, recording, or otherwise, without the written permission of the publisher.

We acknowledge the financial support of the Government of Canada through the Canada Book Fund for business development activities.

5 4 3 2 1   17 16 15 14 13

"The Rosary is my favourite prayer."
—Blessed John Paul II

1. What is the Rosary?

Rooted in the Gospel message, the Rosary is a Christ-centred prayer. Although the prayer is directed to Mary, it is meant to lead us through a meditation on the life, death and resurrection of Jesus Christ. The Rosary walks us through the redemptive work of Jesus, beginning with Mary's "yes" to God and our Lord's conception in Mary's womb – what we call the Incarnation. John Paul II tells us that "to recite the Rosary is nothing other than to contemplate with Mary the face of Christ" (*Rosarium Virginis Mariae*, no. 3).

This public prayer is also meant to be a private prayer, as it draws us into the life of Jesus. Pope Paul VI cautioned that its recitation was not to be "a mechanical repetition of formulas…" (*Marialis Cultus*, 1974, no. 47). Rather, the Rosary is meant to encourage us to relate our own joys and struggles to those of Jesus and those of his mother, Mary. This prayer is meant to be a "compendium of the Gospel." The Rosary draws us into what John Paul II called "Mary's way" because it "is destined to bring forth a harvest of holiness" (*Rosarium Virginis Mariae*, no. 1). In this time-honoured prayer, there is an inseparable bond between Jesus and his mother: "the mysteries of Christ are also in some sense the mysteries of his Mother, even when they do not involve her directly, for she lives from him and through him" (*Rosarium Virginis*

Mariae, no. 24). We can use this prayer to mark the rhythm of daily life as we think about the biblical events that made salvation history. Dominic of Prussia, a fifteenth-century monk, thought of the Rosary as the "Life of Jesus." There is no doubt that our reflection on Mary leads to her son, Jesus Christ.

2 What are the origins of this prayer?

Prayer beads, which are not unique to the Catholic tradition, have been used since pre-Christian times to assist people with prayer and meditation. The original form of the Rosary had 150 beads. This prayer was based on the Psalter, as monks prayed the 150 psalms each week as part of the Liturgy of the Hours. As some lay people and lay monastics were illiterate, they prayed 150 Our Fathers to substitute for the psalms they could not read, using beads to keep count. Eventually, the Hail Mary was included in the prayer and prayed on many of the beads. If beads were not available, a cord with knots was used instead.

There are several accounts of the origins of the Rosary, but John Desmond Miller, author of *Beads & Prayers: The Rosary in History and Devotion,* tells us that "none are complete." By the year 1130, however, we see the recitation of Marian psalters (150 rhymed stanzas, each beginning with the word *Ave*, meaning "Hail") honouring Mary and paraphrasing a thought from the corresponding psalm. Another story of the Rosary describes an encounter between St. Dominic

(d. 1221) and Mary. A story of St. Dominic tells how he was given the Rosary in 1214 and used it to convert the Cathars, a breakaway religious movement.

Tradition notes that the Rosary as we know it evolved over centuries. The prayer known as the *rosarium*, or "rose garden," that began to take shape included introductory prayers and repetition of the Our Father and Hail Mary. The recitation involves meditation on the mysteries of Jesus' life and witness of Mary or "mysteries of salvation."

The structure of the Rosary continued to develop between the twelfth and fifteenth centuries, and by the sixteenth century, the five-decade Rosary was used in devotions. Half of the Hail Mary is based on scripture. By 1160 there were accounts of the beginnings of the full scriptural half of the Hail Mary (Luke 1:28, 42) in some parts of Europe. By this time, the Rosary included the greeting of the angel Gabriel: "Hail Mary, full of grace, the Lord is with you," followed by the Our Father, or Lord's Prayer. Later, the words of St. Elizabeth were added to the Hail Mary: "blessed are you among women." Around the time of the Council of Trent (sixteenth century), the words "Holy Mary, Mother of God, pray for us sinners, now and at the hour of our death" were added. These words are attributed to St. Peter Canisius.

In 1569, official devotion to the Rosary was established by Pope Pius V. October 7 was established as the Feast of Our Lady of Victory; it later changed to the Feast of Our Lady of the Rosary. The Rosary went on to be recommended to faithful Christians; many popes throughout history have supported this devotion. The Rosary had become divided into fifteen brackets, or decades, consisting of ten Hail Marys, and mysteries of faith were assigned to each decade. Somewhere between 1600 and 1700, the Gloria and the Apostles' Creed were added to the recitation of the Rosary.

3 When and how did Blessed John Paul II add to the Rosary?

John Paul II declared October 2002 to October 2003 to be the "Year of the Rosary." He added and defined five new mysteries that are part of a grouping that marks events in the public life and public ministry of Jesus Christ. This new grouping is called the Luminous Mysteries, or the Mysteries of Light.

4 What are the mysteries of the Rosary?

The current form of the Rosary, with the addition of the Luminous Mysteries, is made up of 20 decades of the Hail Mary, separated by an Our Father, Glory Be and sometimes, based on your own preference, the Fatima Prayer. In total, there are four groupings or sets of mysteries. As a general rule, depending on the liturgical season, each set is assigned a day or days of the week for prayer and meditation.

Mysteries	Day of the Week and Liturgical Season
The Joyful Mysteries	Monday and Saturday (and Advent/Christmas)
The Luminous Mysteries	Thursday (and Ordinary Time)
The Sorrowful Mysteries	Tuesday and Friday (and Lent)
The Glorious Mysteries	Wednesday and Sunday (and Easter Season)

⑤ How do I pray the Rosary?

1. Holding the crucifix, begin by blessing yourself, making the Sign of the Cross and reciting the Apostles' Creed:

   I believe in God,
   the Father almighty,
   Creator of heaven and earth,
   and in Jesus Christ, his only Son, our Lord,
   who was conceived by the Holy Spirit,
   born of the Virgin Mary,
   suffered under Pontius Pilate,
   was crucified, died and was buried;
   he descended into hell;
   on the third day he rose again from the dead;
   he ascended into heaven,
   and is seated at the right hand of God
   the Father almighty;
   from there he will come to judge
   the living and the dead.

**I believe in the Holy Spirit,
the holy catholic Church,
the communion of saints,
the forgiveness of sins,
the resurrection of the body,
and life everlasting. Amen.**

2. On the first large bead, pray the Our Father or Lord's Prayer.

   **Our Father, who art in heaven,
   hallowed be thy name;
   thy kingdom come;
   thy will be done on earth as it is in heaven.**

   **Give us this day our daily bread;
   and forgive us our trespasses
   as we forgive those who trespass against us;
   and lead us not into temptation,
   but deliver us from evil. Amen.**

3. On the three smaller beads, pray three Hail Marys. With each bead, pray for an increase in faith, hope and charity – the theological virtues.

   **Hail Mary,
   full of grace,
   the Lord is with thee.
   Blessed art thou among women
   and blessed is the fruit of thy womb, Jesus.**

   **Holy Mary,
   Mother of God,
   pray for us sinners,
   now and at the hour of our death. Amen.**

4. The Glory Be always follows a grouping of small beads. (The Glory Be is also called a Doxology or prayer of praise to God.) Pray the Glory Be prayer:

Glory be to the Father, and to the Son, and to the Holy Spirit. As it was in the beginning, is now, and ever shall be, world without end. Amen.

5. On the next large bead, recite the First Mystery of the set of mysteries you are meditating on, followed by the Our Father. For example, "The First Joyful Mystery is the Annunciation."

6. On the next ten beads, pray a Hail Mary for each one.

7. **Glory be...** (followed by the Fatima Prayer, if you choose to include it):

**O my Jesus, forgive us our sins,
save us from the fires of hell,
lead all souls to heaven,
especially those most in need of thy mercy. Amen.**

8. On the next large bead, recite the second mystery: "The Second Joyful Mystery is the Visitation."

9. Then pray ten Hail Marys.

Continue the pattern until all five mysteries in the grouping have been prayed. After the last Glory Be, pray the Salve Regina or Hail, Holy Queen prayer:

**Hail, holy Queen, Mother of mercy,
hail, our life, our sweetness and our hope.
To thee do we cry, poor banished children of Eve:
to thee do we send up our sighs, mourning and weeping
in this vale of tears.
Turn then, most gracious Advocate,
thine eyes of mercy toward us,**

**and after this our exile,
show unto us the blessed fruit of thy womb,
Jesus, O merciful, O loving, O sweet Virgin Mary!
Pray for us O holy Mother of God,
that we may be made worthy of the promises of Christ.
Amen.**

You may want to have music playing softly in the background as you pray the Rosary. Below I suggest appropriate pieces for each of the four groupings of mysteries.

The Rosary is about holy mysteries and events in the life of Jesus and Mary. As you begin to pray the Rosary, reflect on the many ways in which the lives of Jesus and Mary remind you of key events in your own spiritual journey.

⑥ What are the Joyful Mysteries?

The Joyful Mysteries include stories from Jesus' childhood. These mysteries remind us of the miracle of birth, new beginnings, the joys of family life and the rejoicing in the impossible made real. Saying yes to a new beginning means saying yes to the unknown, to joy, to struggle and to everything in between. Mary celebrates and she worries about her child. Whenever I think of these mysteries, I think of my four children when they were infants. I made up a lullaby that I would sing to them: "Who is my baby boy (girl), Aniello's my baby boy. I love my little baby; Aniello's my baby boy." I would sing these same lines over and over again until they would fall asleep.

♪ Whether you're a parent or not, your favourite lullaby could be the soundtrack for these mysteries. Lullabies remind us of the sweetness associated with parenting and the desire to protect the vulnerable.

The First Joyful Mystery: The Annunciation
(Luke 1:26-33, 38)

The Annunciation marks the event when the Angel Gabriel announces to Mary that she is to be the mother of the messiah. Yet Mary is a virgin and is perplexed about how this can come to be. It is the Holy Spirit that brings about the miraculous conception of Jesus Christ. Mary is amazed at the power of God and how this miracle was communicated through the words of an angel. Mary says yes to God's plan for her, without knowing the demands associated with her "yes." My friend Marilyn once put it this way: "Love says yes." Mary says yes because she loves and trusts God. When it comes to doing God's will, love says yes, but fear says no.

Think about it: Was there ever a time when God amazed you with some tremendous surprise? Were you ever able to do the impossible due to God's grace or holy assistance? Is God calling you to participate in some great mission? Have you said yes? The Angel Gabriel prepared Mary for her mission. How has God prepared you for your own mission?

The Second Joyful Mystery: The Visitation
(Luke 1:39-45)

Mary visits her cousin Elizabeth to celebrate two miraculous pregnancies. Elizabeth and Zechariah had struggled with infertility for a long time; now they are ecstatic that Elizabeth is with child. Two special children are celebrated – John the Baptist and the one for whom John prepares the way: his cousin, our Lord Jesus Christ. Even though this text is a celebration of the good news shared by Mary and Elizabeth, I often wonder whether Mary had gone to visit Elizabeth for comfort and respite. We hear in Matthew's Gospel that Joseph did not believe Mary's story and was tempted to abandon her. The Bible does not tell us how much time elapsed between Joseph's doubt and rejection and his dream, when he is reassured that Mary did not betray him. All we hear is that "just when he had resolved to do this [dismiss her quietly], an angel of the Lord appeared to him in a dream and said, 'Joseph, son of David, do not be afraid to take Mary as your wife, for the child conceived in her is from the Holy Spirit'" (Matthew 1:20). Does Mary go to Elizabeth to rejoice in her good news? Or for emotional and spiritual support? Or both? Is she deeply troubled by Joseph's lack of trust? This mystery encourages us to honour this wonderful relationship, savour the good news of the two pregnancies, and celebrate the gift of friendship and support. Joseph awakens from his physical and spiritual sleep reassured of Mary's goodness. I have often wondered whether this awakening coincided with Mary's return from Elizabeth.

> **Think about it:** Did Mary experience any fear or anxiety after her "yes"? Was she judged and criticized by those in her community? Can you relate to Elizabeth – someone who has had a lifelong desire satisfied after many years of waiting and prayer? ▶

> Are you waiting for a prayer to be answered? Can you relate to Mary – someone who is doing God's will but is being hurt by those closest to her? Can you relate to Joseph – someone who has a hard time trusting God's plan?

The Third Joyful Mystery: The Nativity
(Luke 2:6-12; Matthew 1:25)

We celebrate the birth of Jesus in a stable. Jesus had very humble beginnings. Mary and Joseph were on their way to Bethlehem to be registered when "the time came for her to deliver her child." They had been through quite a journey – the call to be the mother and foster father of the messiah, the pain and distrust that came with this mission, the waiting and adjustment, and finally the need to find a place for a safe delivery. Giving birth to Jesus involved joy and the need for radical trust, but there were good people who celebrated with Mary and Joseph. We relate to those who are the first to hear the good news. The angels do not go first to the learned and the privileged; instead, they go to the shepherds and announce the Messiah's birth. The humble – those considered to be the least of all – were the ones to first hear the good news and visit our Lord. Recalling that the angels spoke first to poor shepherds reminds us that God rewards humility.

> **Think about it:** How have you prepared for the birth of a child? A mission? A project? A marriage? Were you worried about the process or the outcome? Did you trust God with the outcome?

The Fourth Joyful Mystery: The Presentation
(Luke 2:22-36)

Mary and Joseph bring the infant Jesus to the Temple to present him to God. There, Jesus is blessed by two prophets, Simeon and Anna. Simeon takes Jesus in his arms and says to God, "Master, now you are dismissing your servant in peace … for my eyes have seen your salvation…." He then looks to Mary and says, "This child is destined for the falling and the rising of many in Israel, and to be a sign that will be opposed so that the inner thoughts of many will be revealed – and a sword will pierce your own soul too." Simeon knows who Jesus is and is aware of his mission. Apart from many other things, Jesus would be the exposer of lies; this is one of the factors that led to his rejection. Even though Mary and Joseph receive confirmation regarding the identity of Jesus, Mary receives a troubling prophecy. Can you imagine being told of a future pain 30 years before it happens? What did Simeon mean? she may have wondered. Today, we know he was referring to the crucifixion, but what did Mary think about this bittersweet prophecy?

> **Think about it:** Love costs a great deal. When Mary says yes to the glory of being part of Jesus' life, she is included in his mission. Her yes makes this happen. Her yes, however, was not only a yes to the good part, but to all of the sacrifice that goes with loving truth, our loved ones and God. Sometimes loving God costs us, as people may judge us and reject us. Mary was not crucified, but as a mother she experienced a great piercing of the heart. Her cooperation with God's plan involved joy and sacrifice. We know that exposing lies is risky business. ▶

Mary's piercing was related to the cost associated with Jesus' mission. Has your "yes" to God's plan involved some type of suffering? Has your support for a loved one cost you in some way?

The Fifth Joyful Mystery: Finding Jesus in the Temple (Luke 2:41-50)

Mary and Joseph are on their way back from Jerusalem, where they had gone to celebrate the festival of the Passover. After a day or so, they realize that Jesus is missing. We can see how Mary may have thought Jesus was with Joseph or other family members, and Joseph thought he was with Mary. They find him three days later, teaching in the Temple in Jerusalem. Three days is a long time when you are looking for a loved one. Can you imagine the panic and fear that may have seized these frantic parents? Jesus, on the other hand, amazes the crowd with his wisdom and calm.

Think about it: Have you ever waited up at night for your son or daughter to return from a night out with friends? Fear takes over and we may imagine all kinds of crazy scenarios. What if someone hurt my child? Where is she? Why doesn't he call? This passage is a reminder that Mary and Joseph can relate to our day-to-day worries and concerns. This, however, is not the only time Mary would have felt the need to protect her son. Mary and Joseph's flight to Egypt (Matthew 2:13-15) is another example of what parents will endure to keep their children and families safe. Sometimes parents suffer in ways their children may not yet understand. Many refugees can certainly relate to the journey and trials of the Holy Family.

7 What are the Luminous Mysteries?

The Luminous Mysteries, added by John Paul II, are based on the public ministry of Jesus as an adult. The liturgical season of Ordinary Time is a wonderful time to reflect on the mysteries of the life of Jesus: his teaching, his miracles, his travels, his friendships. Recall that before Jesus starts his public ministry, he is tempted for 40 days in the desert. He is tempted with hunger, despair, the desire to test God, and pride. He fasts and prays and is delivered from these temptations. The order in which these temptations appear is not arbitrary. Even though one may be able to resist temptations related to desire and despair, pride is a tough one, because it's all about the preservation of the self. Pride can delay one's spiritual progress as it shifts the focus back to the self and away from God. Have you prayed for self-knowledge, humility and self-discipline before you begin a major project?

> ♪ Enrico Morricone's piece "On Earth as it is in Heaven," from the soundtrack of the film *The Mission*, would be wonderful background music for these mysteries.

The First Luminous Mystery: The Baptism of Jesus (Mark 1:9-11; Luke 3:21-22; Matthew 3:13-17; John 1:29-34)

This mystery ponders the fascinating account of John the Baptist, who baptizes Jesus in the River Jordan. All three persons of the Trinity are revealed to us in this passage: God the Father (the voice), God the Son (Jesus), and God the Holy Spirit (the dove). Jesus models humility for us as he begins his public ministry. John the Baptist, considered a lesser prophet than Jesus, is the one who baptizes Jesus. His was a baptism of conversion. Even though he has no sin, Jesus is open to this process of initiation and shows us the way to perfection because conversion leads to perfection. Later in John's Gospel, John the Baptist says that he must decrease so that Jesus can increase. This is the plan for all of us – to become another Christ. Those parts of us that do not bear spiritual fruit are weeded out by the Holy Spirit to make room for our Lord. In this way, his presence increases.

> **Think about it:** Do you believe that you are a beloved son or daughter of God? Our baptism reminds us of this truth.

The Second Luminous Mystery: The Wedding at Cana (John 2:1-11)

This event marks the first of Jesus' "signs" in the Gospel of John. Jesus and Mary are guests at a wedding in Cana of Galilee when the wine runs out. Mary, no doubt sensing the host's reaction to this turn of events, says to Jesus, "They have no wine." Jesus' response to his mother troubles some people: "Woman, what concern is that to you and to me? My hour has not yet come." Yet Mary says to the others, "Do whatever he tells you." She respects his authority and trusts him, but as his mother, she is sure that he can do something about this situation. I wonder whether Jesus knew that the "hour" of his public ministry had come, but was feeling some anxiety about where it would lead him. Performing this miracle would reveal his identity, and his life and the life of his mother would never be the same. Yet his mother knows it is time for his mission to begin. My friend Anne said that Mary must have given him "that look." We can imagine her thinking, "Come on, you're 30 years old! It's time to get started." She inspires the beginning of his public ministry because she believes in him and in the power of his authority. She knows he is ready. Jesus' power changes the water into wine, and this "revealed his glory." Mary's gentle nudge shows how God needs all of us.

> **Think about it:** St. Paul tells us that he "planted, Apollos watered, but God gave the growth" (1 Corinthians 3:6). Our collaborative efforts support the one plan God has for all of us. Have you ever needed someone to give you a push to start something amazing?

The Third Luminous Mystery: The Proclamation of the Kingdom (Mark 1:14-15)

In this passage, Jesus says, "The time is fulfilled, and the kingdom of God has come near; repent, and believe in the good news." Jesus proclaims the good news of God to everyone – a message that is affirmed throughout the Gospels. People experience the kingdom only after they repent and believe. Repentance implies humility, while belief implies trust. Jesus calls others to join him in the proclamation of the kingdom; in this way, his followers are encouraged to participate in his saving mission.

Think about it: The growth of the kingdom within us depends on the nourishment provided by humility and trust. Take some time to reflect on Jesus' kingdom parables, such as Matthew 13:31-32, and what they mean for us today. Jesus' arrival is connected to the coming of the kingdom.

The Fourth Luminous Mystery: The Transfiguration
(Matthew 17:1-8; Mark 9:2-13; Luke 9:28-36)

Jesus takes Peter, James, and James' brother John with him to a high mountain, where they witness something spectacular: Jesus is transfigured before them. To be transfigured means to be changed into something nobler or more beautiful. Jesus appears to his friends in his glorified state and gives them a sneak preview of himself in the fullness of his glory. Moses and Elijah appear beside him, representing the law and the prophets. The amazement of the Transfiguration is amplified by a voice from heaven: "This is my Son, the Beloved; with him I am well pleased; listen to him!" Jesus' identity is revealed, and God affirms this revelation. Jesus shows us what will happen to us when we, too, receive our glorified bodies in the end times. While the final resurrection of the living and the dead will include the experience of receiving a new body, a glorified body awaits those who are ready to see God. Our ongoing sanctification will bring this about because our bodies are included in God's plan for redemption. The Incarnation is a spectacular reminder of the sanctity of the body. The resurrection involves the restoration of the whole person: body, mind and spirit.

> **Think about it:** Have you ever thought about God's plan for the body? Just as the Transfiguration revealed the glory of Jesus, human and divine, our own sanctification will reveal God's plan for us. Jesus is a sneak preview of God in his divinity and of the restored state of the human person in his humanity. We are familiar with Jesus' question regarding himself: "Who do you say that I am?" We have answered that question in scripture and tradition: Jesus is the Son of God – fully human and fully divine. Nick, one of my students, once said that we should consider this question: "Who does Jesus say that we are?" Do we understand who we are called to be: the restored image and likeness of God?

The Fifth Luminous Mystery: The First Eucharist (Matthew 26:26-28; Mark 14:22-26; Luke 22:14-23; 1 Corinthians 11:23-26)

The Institution of the Eucharist takes place when Jesus celebrates Passover with his disciples. While they are eating, Jesus refers to the bread as his body and the cup of wine as his blood, the "blood of the covenant, which is poured out for many for the forgiveness of sins." This event is the foundation for our belief regarding the Eucharist. *Eucharist* is a Greek word meaning thanksgiving, gratitude, favour or grace. Just as Jesus was human, he was fully divine. What we see is bread and wine, but the Holy Spirit transforms the substance of the bread and wine into the body and blood of Jesus Christ. We trust in this mystery and enter into the paschal mystery each time we celebrate the Eucharist: Christ has died, Christ is risen, Christ will come again. We consume the body of Christ and receive his grace. We receive spiritual nourishment so that we can become another Christ. We also refer to our sharing of the Eucharist as communion or fellowship. We are connected to our brothers and sisters in the Body of Christ when we share of the one body, because Jesus makes us one.

> **Think about it:** Jesus is present in four ways when we celebrate the Mass: in the words of the scriptures, in the presider, in the community of the faithful, and most especially in the Eucharist. We are fed by the written and spoken word, we are fed by the presence of the faithful, and we are fed by the Eucharist. Do you feel Christ's presence feeding you? Does your presence feed others?

8 What are the Sorrowful Mysteries?

These mysteries contain stories of Jesus' suffering and death. They challenge us because they remind us of the reality of human cruelty, the sacrifice of Jesus, and the pain of those who grieve his loss. We relate to these mysteries especially when we suffer due to abuse, emotional or physical pain, grief, betrayal and abandonment.

> ♪ The *Agnus Dei* (Lamb of God) set to Samuel Barber's *Adagio for Strings* would be an appropriate soundtrack for these mysteries.

The First Sorrowful Mystery: The Agony in the Garden (Matthew 26:36-46; Mark 14:32-42; Luke 22:39-46)

This mystery reflects the great tension between our individual free will and God's will. This is especially difficult when we are faced with the possibility of great emotional or physical pain. In the musical *Jesus Christ Superstar*, Jesus refers to the cup as a "cup of poison." Throughout our lives, we need to examine those cups that we choose that are not intended for us or for our fulfillment. God may be saying, "I did not ask you to drink from that cup. I did not ask you to make that choice or take on that new cross." Yet at times, we find ourselves drinking from a bitter cup that we cannot seem to avoid: a new cross has developed in our lives, we are misunderstood, a confrontation needs to take place, a serious illness is diagnosed, or we lose a loved one. The list can go on and on. How many of us ask God to deliver us from these cups? For some reason, known to God alone, there may be times when we are called to drink from them. While we know that Jesus is vindicated and rises from the dead, many of us do not know the outcome of drinking our own "cup." The challenge here is to trust that God's will does not involve our destruction. God is in the restoration business, not the destruction business. God's will involves transformation and new life because God can redeem those painful "agonies" when we feel alone. Since the resurrection vindicates love and truth, God will redeem our sorrows as well. There will be "angels" who sit with us as we wait for restoration. Pain can be harder to bear, however, when our pain is made public.

> **Think about it:** Deitrich Bonhoeffer, in his *Meditations on the Cross*, wrote that it is infinitely easier to suffer publicly with great honour; it is infinitely harder to suffer publicly with great shame. Has the thought of your pain being made public made you vulnerable? Have you ever publicly shamed someone? "Truly I tell you, just as you did it to one of the least of these who are members of my family, you did it to me," Jesus says (Matthew 25:40). Mary was bound up in the public pain of her son. To be public with our pain and vulnerability can be very humbling and difficult, especially when we desire privacy.

The Second Sorrowful Mystery: The Scourging at the Pillar (Mark 15:15)

The Gospels tell us that Jesus was physically beaten and verbally abused throughout his ordeal. Jesus, an innocent man, is misunderstood, betrayed and tortured for proclaiming the truth. When the crowd is asked to choose between Barabbas, a criminal who was in prison for committing murder, and Jesus, the one who healed many and fed the multitudes, the crowd chooses Barabbas. Emotion, misunderstanding, poor judgment and fear have led to this choice. Some of Jesus' actions were misunderstood and criticized. Moreover, Jesus had exposed the sins of many and had challenged those who were arrogant and obnoxious. Those who are challenged in this way, especially if they lack humility and repentance, will resent the one who exposes their lies and weakness. Jesus becomes a scapegoat for the sins of others. Those who fear exposure would rather slander and scapegoat someone else than admit their own guilt. The crowd would rather choose illusion and falsehood than truth, because truth demands humility, sacrifice and the exposure of sins. Many have projected their sins and guilt onto Jesus, and this leads to his suffering and death.

> **Think about it:** If truth threatens, it is either controlled, silenced or killed. Where do you find the strength you need to speak the truth, especially when it is difficult to do so?

The Third Sorrowful Mystery: The Crowning with Thorns (John 19:2)

Not only is Jesus beaten and humiliated, but the Roman soldiers "wove a crown of thorns and put it on his head." No doubt the pain of the thorns pressing into his skull causes him great agony. The blood would have covered his face, obstructing his vision. They mock him, saying, "Hail, King of the Jews!" Humiliation and shame often go hand in hand with abuse – the victim is slandered and shamed as part of the cruelty. The aim is to destroy the person's dignity. Jesus knows how this feels. Unfortunately, for some, this sense of shame can lead to self-loathing. This calls for healing, as some may be convinced that their woundedness and pain is greater than the power and mercy of God. Some may create a "god" of their wound and feel they cannot be redeemed or made whole. Jesus shows us that redemption and restoration are possible. God's love and mercy are greater than any wound that holds us hostage. We do not have to choose weakness and struggle, for we can choose Christ, who is in us.

Think about it: Whenever I meditate on this mystery, I pray for all people who are experiencing mental illness. The inability to perceive correctly, whether it is due to biological, social or psychological factors, can be disabling. Victims of torture and abuse should be remembered here as well. Our prayers can help them as we ask God to restore their joy and peace. Jesus uses the Aramaic word for "debt" when he refers to sin. He uses the language of currency when he talks about forgiveness and reconciliation. Whenever I hurt someone, I take something from that person: his or her peace or joy. Reconciliation involves restoring that which has been lost or taken, and can bring us peace.

The Fourth Sorrowful Mystery: The Carrying of the Cross (Mark 15:31-32)

The scourging leaves open wounds on Jesus' back. The wood of the cross presses into these sores. The Gospel writers tell us that Simon of Cyrene is asked to help Jesus and carries the cross part of the way. Simon is an example of how we can join our own pain and losses to those of Jesus. Simon's assistance gave Jesus some relief during this excruciating ordeal. Our loved ones walk with us whenever we face a life-threatening journey. Our crosses involve them, too. We suffer in ways unique to us, and those who love us suffer in ways unknown to us.

Think about it: Has a loving act of kindness given you relief in times of distress? Can we discern those crosses we are not to carry? Sometimes our good intentions, our desire to protect our loved ones, to cover up for their mistakes or to carry their ▶

> crosses may lead to a delay in their own conversion process. Our kindness may be an obstacle to the growth of another; therefore, we must pray for courage to allow some of our loved ones to work through their own challenges. If we continue to rescue them over and over again, valuable life lessons may be lost and we may find ourselves with far too many crosses. Pray for the wisdom to know the difference. Sometimes we are to be like Simon, when assisting someone with their cross is all about the offer of relief. At other times, it's about the fear associated with seeing our loved ones suffer due to consequences. Living through the fallout, however, may be their only salvation.

The Fifth Sorrowful Mystery: The Crucifixion
(John 19:25-30)

This mystery takes our breath away. How could this happen? Who is responsible? How do Jesus' friends feel? How does his mother manage such pain? Do those who shouted, "Crucify him!" feel any regret? Even though the centurion remarked, "Certainly this man was innocent" (Luke 23:47), those who were supposed to defend him abandoned him. When someone is taken from us prematurely, or due to the sins of others, such as through an act of violence, we find ourselves in shock, disillusioned. Crucifixion is a brutal form of corporal punishment and was used only on non-Roman citizens, because it was such a shameful kind of execution. Jesus' loved ones must have wailed at the sight of his pain, reduced to thoughts of despair and confusion. Mary is left in the land of the living with her own emotional crucifixion. "And a sword will pierce your own soul too," Simeon had said to her at the beginning. Jesus is crucified and Mary's heart is crushed.

> **Think about it:** Grief is an emotion that we must work through. We feel it in our bodies and in our spirits. The raw moments that follow a death are paralyzing. Death separates us from our loved ones; we are left with the challenge to trust and believe that the separation is temporary; our faith reminds us that we will see our loved ones again. For every person who suffers the brutality of an agonizing death, there is another person who suffers the agony of a pierced heart – the ripple effect of pain.

⑨ What are the Glorious Mysteries?

Now we have come full circle. Jesus came from God and returns to God in his glorified, resurrected body. Truth and love are vindicated and God's justice is restored. Truth can never die. Life is eternal. The Glorious Mysteries remind us that not every day, week, month or year will be like the difficult ones. Pain can be redeemed, and we are promised eternal life with God and our loved ones. God's love shines through the resurrection as we witness the power of the Holy Spirit.

> ♪ The closing piece of Paco Peña's *Missa Flamenca* would be a lovely soundtrack for these mysteries, full of celebration and sounds of triumph.

The First Glorious Mystery: The Resurrection
(Matthew 28:1-10; Mark 16:1-8; Luke 24:1-12; John 20:1-10)

The resurrection is the miracle that affirms Jesus' identity and the truth that we are eternal beings – that life continues after death. It is the ultimate relief after a heavy burden is lifted. When Jesus resuscitates Lazarus, he tells Lazarus's sister, Mary, "I am the resurrection and the life. Those who believe in me, even though they die, will live, and everyone who lives and believes in me will never die. Do you believe this?" (John 11:25-26). Even though we wait for the final resurrection of the living and the dead in the last days, we can experience mini-resurrections when our lives are turned around and we become new persons in Christ. The resurrection gives the grieving person hope: hope for reconciliation with our deceased loved ones. The resurrection gave Jesus' mother and his disciples the spark and courage they needed to spread the word about the life and ministry of Jesus. Jesus lives! Only things that are of God have true power over us. Humility allows the power of God to shine through. In John's empty tomb account, we hear that Mary Magdalene thought that Jesus was the gardener (John 20:11-18). Even in his resurrected state, Jesus models humility. He could have appeared as a majestic king in velvet robes and jewels, but he chose to present himself as a humble gardener – the gardener of life who removes weeds and prunes branches.

> **Think about it:** The deeper meaning of the resurrection is that any obstacle can be overcome. The death of Jesus is overcome by God's power and love – the cross conquers sin and the resurrection conquers death. Here we experience a shift from fear to courage and restoration. God redeems different parts of our lives in manageable stages until our lives our restored. Does the resurrection account give you hope in your grief? Do you believe you will see your loved ones again?

The Second Glorious Mystery: The Ascension
(Mark 16:19-20; Luke 24:50-53; Acts 1:9)

After his earthly mission, Jesus returns to God in heaven. During his earthly life, Jesus experienced great intimacy with God. By calling God "Abba" many times, Jesus communicated a loving and nurturing relationship. "Abba" is an intimate term for a father, like "Daddy." Jesus shows us the way back to the Father. We, too, can experience the beatific vision, or union with God. This process can start in this lifetime. When we surrender all of our thoughts, habits and actions to the power of the Holy Spirit, they can be transformed and can give glory to God. Jesus wants us to participate in the same intimate relationship he has with his Heavenly Father.

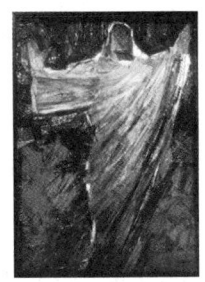

> **Think about it:** It is amazing to think of Jesus in heaven with his glorified body. This remains a mystery for us. The resurrection and the Ascension have deep spiritual significance for our lives: not only do they represent restoration, they also represent release – release from pain, guilt and bondage. They represent the person in his or her most awakened state. The body – once it is surrendered to the power of the Holy Spirit to be, as St. Paul teaches, a temple of the Holy Spirit – becomes a wonderful manifestation of the glory of God. We give glory to God in our bodies and in our minds. Jesus heals the whole person so that our minds can perceive correctly and our bodies can reveal the wonder and awe of the Lord. Do you believe and trust that God loves you? God does not add or delete love. God is love and his love endures forever (1 John 4:7, 8).

The Third Glorious Mystery: The Descent of the Holy Spirit (Acts 2:1-7, 11)

The feast of Pentecost marks the beginning of the Church. Those disciples who had been paralyzed with fear were released from bondage. The Holy Spirit descended like tongues of fire on the disciples, and they received the strength they needed to go out and spread the good news of Jesus Christ. St. Paul and the other apostles set up churches in many places; Christians began to gather to be baptized, to break bread together, to pray, to worship and to enjoy fellowship. The Holy Spirit continues the saving work of Jesus Christ, just as Jesus promised. It is the Holy Spirit that sanctifies us and transforms us into the restored image and likeness of God.

> **Think about it:** Have you taken some time to review the gifts of the Holy Spirit you studied when you prepared to receive the sacrament of Confirmation (Isaiah 11:2-3)? Have you reflected on St. Paul's theology of the gifts of the Holy Spirit (1 Corinthians 12:4-13; 14:3)? We are one body with many members who build up the body of Christ by using our gifts. Using these gifts will bear great spiritual fruit (Galatians 5:22-24). Your mission is unique – there is only one of you.

The Fourth Glorious Mystery: The Assumption of Mary (Tradition)

In the early Church, this feast was known as the "Dormition" or the "falling asleep" of Mary. Tradition, which is based on liturgy, art, a strong oral tradition, and the writings of early Christian writers, tells us that at the end of her earthly life,